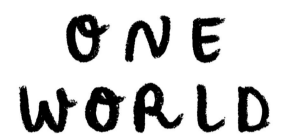

# ONE WORLD

## 24 HOURS ON PLANET EARTH

# ONE WORLD

## 24 HOURS ON PLANET EARTH

NICOLA DAVIES

illustrated by
JENNI DESMOND

CANDLEWICK PRESS

GREENWICH, LONDON

# A NOTE TO THE READER

Planet Earth, our home, is always turning. One whole turn is what we call a day. Imagine the Earth divided into twenty-four segments like an orange; the time it takes for Earth to spin through one of those segments is what we call an hour.

By international agreement, the first segment begins on a line that passes through the city of London, England; this line runs around our planet, from pole to pole. When it's midnight in London (12:00 a.m. Greenwich Mean Time, or GMT), it's also the start of a new hour in every other one of the segments around the world.

In practice, most time zones aren't straight segments, as each country determines how the clocks should be set within their borders. Some regions observe Daylight Savings Time as well, which further complicates things! In this book, we've treated each segment as an hour in order to highlight the steady march of the day as the Earth turns.

So read on to take a trip around the world and see what's happening on Planet Earth in just one moment . . .

## APRIL 21: ONE MINUTE TO MIDNIGHT
## GREENWICH, LONDON, UK

Where on Earth are you right now? Maybe where you are it's time for breakfast, or maybe it's time for bed. It's late where I am, and almost everyone's asleep, but I'm awake, looking out into the night. Wondering.

Wondering what's happening on Earth right now, when far to the east it's already morning and far to the west it's still just afternoon.

Why don't we go together, you and I, and see—just as the clock starts striking midnight.

BONG!

SVALBARD, ARCTIC CIRCLE (1 a.m.)

The spring sun is shining in the middle of the Arctic night—and it won't set until September. Look out there, on the frozen sea: a mother polar bear is hunting seals to feed her two small cubs.

Every year now the ice melts earlier, making hunting hard. The future of this little family is not certain.

**BONG!** 🕛 **LUANGWA VALLEY, ZAMBIA (2 a.m.)**

See there, among the tree-trunk legs of Mom and Granny, aunts and sisters? A newborn elephant, wobbling to her feet. Lion roars may split the night, but her family will protect her—and wildlife rangers will do their best to protect them *all* from poachers, who would like to kill these elephants and sell their tusks.

Watch where you put your feet! Baby sea turtles are wriggling from their eggs beneath the sand. Don't shine your flashlight, because the light will confuse them; they look for the bright line of the horizon to steer themselves toward the sea.

Many beaches where sea turtles lay their eggs are threatened by pollution or by humans who use the eggs for food. But here they are protected, guarded by wildlife rangers, and many hatchlings make it to the sea.

BONG!

12 ↑ GMT

## GAOLIGONGSHAN NATIONAL NATURE RESERVE, CHINA (6:30 a.m.)

First light is the cue for gibbons to start their song. Listen: that's the female whooping. Next, her mate joins her in a wild duet, which says, "This is our home."

Lower down the mountain, all the trees have been cut down. But up here, gibbon families still sing from night to day . . . sending pangolins and clouded leopards off to bed and waking birds and monkeys.

BONG!

12
GMT

# DONSOL, PHILIPPINES (8 a.m.)

Twenty whale sharks, cruising slowly in the warm blue water! All gulping plankton into mouths the size of trash cans, feasting on a soup of tiny creatures.

No one knows exactly where the whale sharks come from, but each one's spotty pattern is as unique as a fingerprint—and by studying them, scientists know that more than six hundred different sharks come here to feast. Finding out more about these amazing creatures will help these scientists to protect whale sharks.

**BONG!** 12 ↑ GMT **MUTAWINTJI NATIONAL PARK, AUSTRALIA (10 a.m.)**

Phew . . . it's hot! The mob is in the shade beneath the gum trees; flyers and their joeys graze. It's another scorching day—even hotter and drier lately than kangaroos are used to, with the bushfires getting worse and their water holes drying up. But two big boomers are still squaring up for a fight. They groan and grunt, push and wrestle, until the older one balances on his tail and kicks so hard that the younger staggers back. He lopes away . . .

not yet ready to take the old kangaroo's crown!

BONG!
ROSS ISLAND, ANTARCTICA (12 noon)

It will soon be winter in Antarctica; in two days, the sun will set for five whole months. That's why the emperor penguins have arrived: they need sea ice to find a mate and raise a chick.

The ice is melting, and life is getting harder for these birds. But emperors are survivors— and human beings can help them by protecting their feeding grounds from boats and fishing.

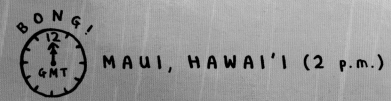

Like a mountain shooting through the surface, then the biggest SPLASH you've ever seen! That was a humpback whale breaching. Soon the whales will be heading to Alaska for a long summer.

Once, whales like this were hunted until they almost disappeared, but now they're doing well—which proves human beings can learn to change.

The afternoon is warm and the air's alive with buzzing: bees as small as
sesame seeds and as big as almonds; hummingbirds with backs like emeralds.
There are flowers here to suit them all . . . It's an oasis of blossom and buzz, where
they can thrive safe from the chemicals that have made them rare on farmland.
The bees and hummingbirds bring pollen to our crops—without them,
human beings would have no fruits or vegetables!

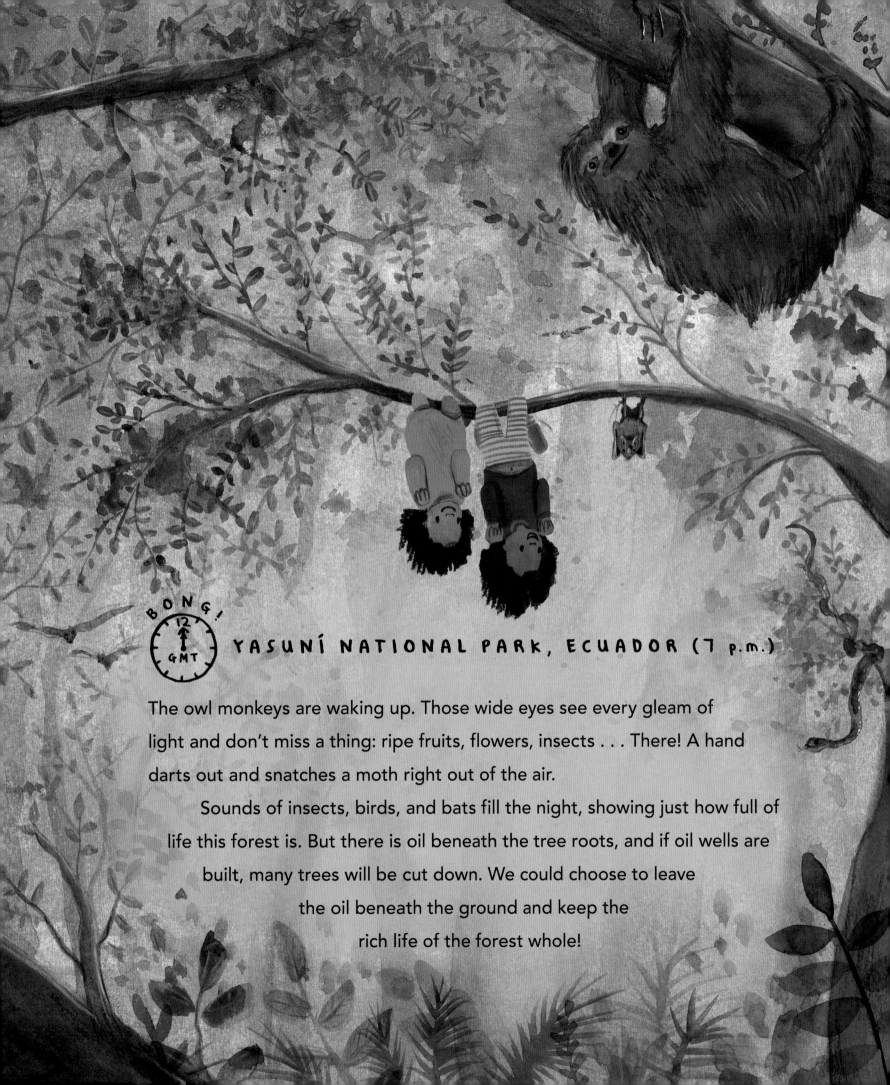

BONG!

**YASUNÍ NATIONAL PARK, ECUADOR (7 p.m.)**

The owl monkeys are waking up. Those wide eyes see every gleam of
light and don't miss a thing: ripe fruits, flowers, insects . . . There! A hand
darts out and snatches a moth right out of the air.

Sounds of insects, birds, and bats fill the night, showing just how full of
life this forest is. But there is oil beneath the tree roots, and if oil wells are
built, many trees will be cut down. We could choose to leave
the oil beneath the ground and keep the
rich life of the forest whole!

*Shhhh.* There, along the riverbank: a jaguar! It swims without disturbing the stars' reflections, creeps up to the caiman . . . pounces . . . *bites.*

Sometimes jaguars will kill farmers' cows—then farmers kill jaguars. And there are so few left! That's why, in Brazil, some farmers are switching to keeping cows related to Spanish fighting bulls, which can stand up to jaguars and send them running. This keeps the ranchers happy and the jaguars safe.

BONG!

BIRD ISLAND, SOUTH GEORGIA (10 p.m.)

Far, far south again, for the very last stop. See how the albatross chick huddles in the nest,
against the wind and storm? She's been alone for days while her mom and dad fly over the
ocean to find her food.

Her parents could get caught on fishing lines and never come back—or mistake plastic
for food and bring home bottle tops and pull tabs for her to eat. But not tonight!
Look: here comes Dad with a dinner of squid to share!

The last chime of midnight has sounded—
it's time to go. Back over ocean, where plastic
clogs the waves; back over land, where human roads
stretch into the distance and city lights pierce
the night . . . where fires burn and, everywhere,
signs show the world is getting warmer.

## THE FIRST HOUR OF APRIL 22: EARTH DAY
## GREENWICH, LONDON, UK

The final stroke of midnight has rung out. But think of all the wonders that we've seen, and the millions of others that we haven't, which exist in every moment, every day.

I can feel them out there, everywhere. Can't you? They're part of us and every breath we take. Our world is fragile and threatened—but still lovely. And now it's the start of a new day—a day when I'll speak about these wonders, shout them out . . .

and tell the sleepers to **WAKE UP**

because tomorrow is already here.

## A NOTE FROM THE AUTHOR

To write this book I had to do a lot of research and think carefully about the time of year to choose, because every natural event in the story is rooted in reality. Quite by chance, late April had exciting things happening in every time zone—which is why I imagine the events in the book unfolding on the night before April 22, when Earth Day has been celebrated around the world since 1970.

The story you have just read began and ended at midnight; all of the action, in all of the habitats we visited around the world, took place between the first and last chimes of the clock. Of course, there is a double meaning here: our climate is changing, the clock has struck, and it is time to make a difference together. And so, Jenni Desmond and I wanted this book to be both a joyful celebration of our home planet and a call to action to save all the loveliness that is still out there . . . right this minute . . .

## A NOTE FROM THE ARTIST

Creating these illustrations during the global pandemic meant I really related to the girls in their room, who went outside only in their imagination. I loved joining them, on the boundary of yesterday and tomorrow, to look at the beautiful world outside, full of wonderful animals and extraordinary landscapes. I adventured and explored the Earth by their side, and I hope you will enjoy exploring it with them, too.

Today more and more people are sitting up and taking notice of climate change and starting to take action. Nicola Davies's words highlight the difficulties that different ecosystems and animals are experiencing, and we hope this book brings awareness and hope for our future together on our beautiful, fragile planet.

# WHAT IS CLIMATE CHANGE?

The air that surrounds you right now is part of what we call the Earth's atmosphere: a layer of gases that stretches from the ground to more than 60 miles (100 kilometers) above your head and that protects us from the cold of outer space. But human beings have burned so much coal, oil, and gas to make energy to run our homes, farms, cities, cars, planes, and trains that the mixture of gases in the atmosphere has changed.

Now there is too much of a gas called carbon dioxide in the air, which affects the balance and means that Earth's atmosphere has trapped too much heat. As a result, the planet is getting warmer. THIS is climate change, and it's causing unusual weather of all kinds, which makes life more difficult for both animals and people. Storms are bigger, floods and droughts happen more often, and the ice at the North and South Poles is melting, so that the sea levels are rising.

# WHAT CAN PEOPLE DO TO HELP?

All around the world, people of all ages are working to make a difference about climate change. Lots of things we do in our ordinary lives use energy and add to the carbon dioxide that is in the atmosphere . . . but the good news is that there are little ways families can help by doing things like using less energy at home, turning off lights when they aren't needed, and not wasting food or water.

You can talk to your parents and teachers and see what ideas you can come up with together: for example, you could ask if your school gets electricity from a company that uses solar, wind, or wave power, or do something to support an organization that protects the environment and helps take carbon dioxide out of the air. Most important of all is to tell other people what you know about climate change and what they can also do to help!

To the staff of the World Land Trust and
all their partners around the world who work hard
to protect the wild and all its beauty
**N D**

For my Josie.  And for the start of a new day.
**J D**

First edition 2023

Library of Congress Catalog Card Number 2022907001
ISBN 978-1-5362-2613-3

23 24 25 26 27 APS 10 9 8 7 6 5 4 3 2

Printed in Humen, Dongguan, China

This book was typeset in Avenir.
The illustrations were done in mixed media.

Candlewick Press
99 Dover Street
Somerville, Massachusetts 02144

www.candlewick.com